PRIVATE PLACEMENT LIFE INSURANCE

A Sophisticated Investment Solution for High Net Worth Investors

3 DIMENSIONAL
WEALTH ADVISORY

By
Gerald R. Nowotny
and
Monroe "Roey" Diefendorf, Jr.

Table of Contents

Private Placement Life Insurance (PPLI)

Purpose

This report is designed to provide high net worth investors that invest in potential high return / high turnover funds with an overview of the benefits and potential uses of private placement life insurance ("PPLI"). Most fund-of-fund offerings are tax inefficient primarily generating income that is taxed as ordinary income.

The tax horizon continues to look turbulent. The top federal marginal tax bracket is 39.6 percent. An additional Medicare tax of 3.8 percent also applies for married taxpayers with adjusted gross income (AGI) of $250,000. On top of that, add on your state and local income taxes (i.e. NYS - 8.82% & NYC – 3.876%) and an investor can be paying at a marginal rate of over 56%! The rate for qualified dividends returns to the normal rate for ordinary income. The long-term capital gains rate is now at 20%. With regards to estate taxes, the top marginal federal bracket is 40% with the exemption equivalent for 2015 at a level of $5,430,000.

Introduction

The use of the phrase "good investment" with life insurance has long been an oxymoron. Retail life insurance agents have sold permanent life insurance contracts as "private retirement" vehicles. A whole selling system using permanent life insurance eschewing the use of qualified retirement and IRAs proliferated amongst life insurance agents. Traditional life insurance products have been too laden with heavy front-end sales charges and limited investment flexibility for sophisticated buyers such as high net worth individuals and large institutions. This selling phenomenon occurred in spite of the significant tax-advantages that life insurance enjoys in comparison to other financial products.

The evolution of the PPLI marketplace for high net worth individuals has its origins with hedge fund investors. The sophisticated hedge fund investor whose yields are regularly driven down by the substantial tax rates imposed on ordinary income and short-term capital gains is acutely aware of the tax inefficiency of hedge funds. Hedge fund managers have attempted to utilize various investment swaps to convert a portion of the investment income into long-term capital gains income; however, none of these strategies offers the comprehensive tax-advantages of PPLI.

Tax Advantages of Life Insurance

Life insurance has enjoyed significant tax advantages for a life time period. In general, life insurance offers five distinct tax benefits:

- Tax-deferred "inside build-up" of policy cash values.
- Non-recognition of capital gains. Ability to switch investment options within the product without triggering taxation.
- Option of tax-free access to policy cash values through a partial surrender of the cash value and low cost policy loans.
- Income tax-free death benefits.
- Estate tax-free death benefits through the use of third party ownership of the policy such as an irrevocable life insurance trust ("ILIT").

The original legislative intent behind these tax-advantages is rooted in social policy designed to encourage household savings and insurance protection for "widows and orphans". Over the course of time, those tax advantages have remained steadfastly in place. The tax rules for life insurance make no distinction between income and net worth levels of the policyholder. Large corporations and banks have exploited permanent life insurance for the same reasons to the extent of investments that well exceed $100 billion.

The insurance industry has fiercely guarded these long-standing benefits that are written in the Internal Revenue Code ("IRC" or "Code") over the years through a well-organized and funded lobbying effort by the American Council of Life Insurers ("ACLI"). Life insurance agents also have a well-funded and organized lobby that has effectively preserved the tax advantages of life insurance.

Development of PPLI

High net worth individuals have long realized the potential opportunities of life insurance as a "tax- advantaged" investment. The primary negatives have been the high-end front-loaded sales loads associated with traditional permanent life insurance contracts – whole life, universal life and indexed universal life, as well as the absence of investment flexibility.

Products such as whole life insurance and universal life insurance are representative of traditional general account life insurance products. Traditional general account life insurance products produce conservative investment results. The policy's investment return or crediting rate is tied to the investment return of the insurer's general account assets.

The investments of the general account are restricted by statute and are primarily comprised of investment grade bonds and mortgages. General account investments tend to be liquid as the life insurer's risk based capital ratio as measured by independent rating agencies who consider investment liquidity, as well as investment risk and quality as part of its assessment of the life insurance.

General account products have been primarily distributed through the general agency system for most of the last century. These products were designed for mass distribution and carry high front-end sales loads, which provide an adverse drag on the investment performance of the general account policies. As a result, these products have had little investment appeal to the sophisticated long- term investor in spite of any tax advantage that the product might offer. In the typical retail life insurance contract, the policy's cumulative premiums normally do not exceed the policy's cash value until after the policy's 8th or 9th year. Most universal life insurance contracts feature declining surrender charges which last from 10-15 years within the policy.

The introduction and distribution of Variable Universal Life insurance ("VUL") increased dramatically over the decades of the 1980's and 1990's in the wake of the Bull Market. Sales of VUL comprised 40 to 50% of life insurance company sales. VUL is a separate account product, which offers multiple investment options in a manner similar to mutual funds.

Assets of the separate account are not subject to the creditors of the insurer in the event of default. The investment performance of these investment funds is a direct pass-through to the policyholder and allows the policyholder to participate in various investment markets. However, the sophisticated investor is still limited to the investment selections of the insurer as well as the presence of high front-end sales loads.

The advent of PPLI began around 1992 -1993 following the use of similar products (without hedge funds) by large corporations. Al Block, a substantial corporate owned life insurance (COLI) producer, placed the first high net worth policies with CIGNA. The offshore PPLI marketplace developed in the 1995-1996 around two separate and distinct themes. Wealthy families emigrating to the U.S. used PPLI and private variable deferred annuity (PPVA) contracts as part of their "in bound" tax planning. Tremont developed a small Bermuda-based life insurance company around the same time.

PPLI policies were created with this issue in mind, namely; *"How does the high net worth investor combine the strong tax advantages of life insurance with a life insurance product that offers customized investment options for the sophisticated investor in a product that is institutionally priced?"*

The assets of PPLI are not subject to the claims of the insurer in the event of the insurer's default in any of the domestic jurisdictions as well as the principal offshore jurisdictions in the PPLI marketplace (Bermuda, Cayman Islands, and Puerto Rico). Access to this type of product in the high net worth marketplace has been available for the last twelve to fourteen years. PPLI had previously been available in the corporate marketplace with very high minimum premiums. The marketplace has changed in the last several years to make PPLI available at a lower premium threshold.

PPLI is an institutionally priced VUL with customized investment options. The product is only available to accredited investors and qualified purchasers as defined in federal securities law. The product is offered by the insurer through a private placement memorandum (PPM), which fully discloses all of the costs associated with the policy as well as the policy's provisions. The policy has sales loads, which are dramatically lower than retail life products reflecting the institutional pricing of the product.

Though the primary attraction of PPLI for the high net worth investor might be the combination of the tax advantages along with the institutional pricing and investment flexibility, PPLI offers the same utility of any other permanent life insurance contract to meet important tax and investment planning objectives. In a VUL policy, the owner enjoys income tax deferred growth of capital during the life of the insured. In addition, the product provides the named beneficiary(ies) of the policy with an income tax-free death benefit payment upon the death of the insured.

If the ownership is properly structured for estate tax purposes, significant gift and estate tax savings can be generated. The policy can be utilized to provide the estate/beneficiaries of the investor with increased liquidity that can be utilized for a variety of purposes. For example, death proceeds may be used for the payment of estate taxes that may be imposed on the significant other assets that such an investor may have accumulated over a lifetime.

U.S. vs. Offshore PPLI

Domestic PPLI

PPLI is available in both the domestic and offshore marketplaces. Over the last ten years, high net worth PPLI has become more of a domestic market. The two leading life insurers are Philadelphia Financial Life Assurance Company (PFLAC) and American General. Over the last two years, several large life insurers have left the marketplace; Sun Life of Canada, Nationwide, New York Life and MassMutual. In addition, while substantial resources are required, smaller carriers are making their entrance into the market, such as Investor Preferred Life of Rapid City, South Dakota.

The decision of which offering to purchase, domestic or offshore, is a function of personal tax planning needs. Generally, the domestic offering for a U.S. taxpayer provides coverage through an institutional quality carrier with a long track record, independent third party ratings and extensive regulatory oversight by the various states and industry groups. The domestic carrier may be able to accommodate a much larger policy investment due to the greater availability of reinsurance.

The only limiting factor in this investment concept is the availability of reinsurance. The current market cap on a single life is $65 million. The policy must satisfy the tax definition of life insurance under IRC Sec. 7702 in order to preserve the tax advantages. These definitions, the cash value accumulation test or the guideline premium/cash value corridor test, envision a certain ratio of death benefit to cash value depending upon the age of the insurer. The availability of reinsurance is two to four times greater in the domestic market than the offshore market.

A trade-off in the domestic market is the imposition of a state premium tax. State premium taxes vary between 1.75% (175 bps) to 3.75% (375 bps) depending upon the state. However, South Dakota has instituted an extremely low premium tax of only 0.008% (8 bps). This is a very important feature when deciding upon which jurisdiction your PPLI is established. In addition, a federal tax, known as the DAC (Deferred Acquisition Cost), is an additional cost within the product. The carrier will typically amortize this tax through a 1.00% -

1.50% premium load within the product.

Domestic PPLI offerings have minimized the importance of offshore options, as well as the increased compliance requirements required for offshore investments.

Offshore life insurance is subject to the reporting requirements of the Foreign Bank Account Reporting Act (FBAR) in the event the cash value exceeds $10,000, which requires a taxpayer to file TDF 90.22.1 no later than June 30th. The Foreign Account Tax Compliance Act also became effective on January 1, 2013.

Several offshore life insurers have created Puerto Rican life insurance subsidiaries in response to these compliance requirements. Puerto Rico as a U.S. Commonwealth is not subject to FBAR and FACTA.

Offshore PPLI

The asset protection opportunities available in certain tax-haven jurisdictions may point the investor towards an offshore purchase. Generally, most offshore life insurance jurisdictions have adopted separate account legislation, which exempts the separate account assets from the claims of the insurer. The policy is also exempt from the claims of the policyholder. Tax haven jurisdictions have adopted sophisticated trust legislation to protect the assets of a trust. These jurisdictions such as Nevis and the Cook Islands, combine a short statute of limitations with a very high burden of proof on creditors along with a legal policy not to recognize foreign judgments.

From an insurance standpoint, the difference in the insurance regulatory environment provides the opportunity to offer PPLI with investment options, which are less liquid. Investment options within a VUL may be restricted in the domestic marketplace to the extent that they provide little liquidity. Offshore PPLI may provide access to non-SEC approved offshore investments, which are unavailable in the United States.

All states have adopted non-forfeiture laws, which require paying the policyholder in cash within a six month period from the time of notification for policy loan, or surrenders. Similarly, most states have adopted statutes with respect to the timeliness of the death benefit payment. Generally, death benefit payment made after a 30-day period carries an interest penalty, which can be as high as 12 percent.

While many states would allow a delayed payment through a policy endorsement such as an in kind death benefit of the limited partner interest, Rev. Rul. 2003-91 and Rev. Rul. 2003-92 have placed in question the ability to use this endorsement. While an offshore insurance regulator would allow for much greater flexibility in this area, the in kind benefit is still subject to the same federal tax considerations regarding the Investor Control Doctrine.

As a result, domestic and offshore life insurers have opted for a deferred payment endorsement. Depending upon the jurisdiction, a life insurer may have the ability to delay payment for six months up to an indefinite amount of time. Offshore PPLI may allow investment options, such as private placement offerings for venture capital, private equity, and leveraged buyout, which tend to have longer "lock up" periods. Domestic carriers will frequently only allow a "lock up" and payment deferrals of up to one year. These investment offerings are generally highly illiquid. Many states have approved carrier endorsements for deferred payment on policy benefits. Of note is

South Dakota, where in kind death benefit payments are allowable and provide an attractive alternative to offshore PPLI.

The offshore PPLI acquisition may also confer a cost savings through avoidance of a state premium tax. State premium taxes generally average 1.75% (175 bps) to 3.75% (375 bps) of the premium. Avoidance of the state premium tax may constitute a 15-20-basis advantage on the return over the long-term. Generally, a U.S. taxpayer or a policy with U.S. beneficiaries should purchase, which is compliant with IRC Section 7702, through an insurer which has made an IRC Section 953(d) election.

The IRC Section 953(d) election is corporate election, which allows the insurer to be treated as a U.S. taxpayer. This election avoids income tax withholding on certain categories of investment income such as dividends, portfolio interest, rents and royalties. This election removes the risk of the carrier being "dragged" onshore as a U.S trade or business since it is insuring U.S. lives.

In the event an offshore life insurer suffered an adverse result on a tax audit, the risk to the policyholder is the risk that the policy would need to be re-priced for U.S. corporate taxes. This result could have a devastating impact on the policyholder. As a result, a U.S taxpayer should purchase a policy from an insurer, which has made this election.

A non-resident may also purchase PPLI from an offshore carrier. The policy need not be U.S. tax compliant. As a result, the policy can maintain a minimal ratio of death benefit-to-cash value. Generally, European-styled unit linked policies have a death benefit which is 101% to 110% of the cash value. Most jurisdictions around the world confer tax-advantaged treatment to life insurance, and many countries are adopting the concept of worldwide taxation.

These policies do not require a carrier, which has made the IRC section 953(d) election. The non-resident would generally need a policy issued by a carrier that has made an IRC Sec 953(d) election, if the investment income is subject to withholding taxes. Additionally, investment income that would be treated as effectively connected income to a U.S. trade or business (ECI) is better suited within a policy issued by an IRC

Sec 9539(d) electing carrier.

Due to the small numbers of reinsurers operating in the offshore high net worth PPLI marketplace, the availability of reinsurance for large premium investments is roughly 2 to 3 times greater in the domestic market. While it is widely believed that that the pricing of offshore policies is more competitive than domestic policies, this claim may not be true. The offshore markets have few carriers in general and even fewer institutional quality carriers. The competition among institutional quality carriers is not as great as in the domestic marketplace.

Bermuda and Cayman Islands are the primary offshore jurisdiction for offshore insurers. Both have a long stable history both politically and economically. In choosing an offshore situs, political and economic stability are critical factors.

PPLI and Its Impact on Estate and Wealth Preservation Planning

The sophisticated investor can benefit by employing the life insurance policy of the VUL contract to his or her Registered Investment Advisory investments in a manner that can promote a significantly higher net "after-tax" return on investment. The concept of PPLI is a relatively new development in the world of Insurance Dedicated Funds (IDF) for the Registered Investment Advisors (RIA). However, it is not difficult to understand that if there is a way to structure a particular investment within a tax advantaged life insurance policy; the fund's regular investors will be much better served on a total return basis.

As described above, the PPLI incorporates RIA investment strategies into its chassis which become the policy's cash values. The policies are designed to provide a sufficient amount of insurance death benefit in order to comply with the requirements of the United States Internal Revenue Code definition of life insurance (IRC Sec 7702) (as opposed to characterization as an investment policy or annuity) and to provide a minimal increase in the actual death benefit in excess of the cash value account accumulation. The chart found on page 22 depicts an example of such a policy design and affords a simple contrast to that of a taxable investment.

In the following example, we have assumed a

healthy, non-smoker 50-year old male investing $10 million in an investment earning 8% per year after management fees. The marginal tax rate is assumed to be 47% (federal, state and local). The policy is a modified endowment contract ("MEC"), which uses the guideline premium/cash value corridor definition of life insurance.

This investment is compared to a similar deposit into a hypothetical PPLI policy. As the chart indicates, the cost of the "tax advantaged" IDF is substantially lower than the cost of paying income taxes. The illustrated results project a total cost of 138 basis points in the early years dropping to approximately 80 basis points over time as the "price tag" to avoid income tax. Among items that may affect this illustration are the actual age and health of the insured, investor's actual marginal tax rate and the actual performance of the IDF.

Male Age 50 - $10.0 Million

HYPOTHETICAL ILLUSTRATION

Year	Net Taxable Investment Value	End of Year Policy Cash Value	Death Benefit	Net Taxable Investment IRR	Policy Cash Value IRR	Death Benefit IRR
1	10,795,000	11,362,510	35,943,930	7.95%	13.62%	259.44%
2	11,653,203	12,912,620	35,943,930	7.95%	13.62%	89.60%
3	12,579,632	14,684,290	35,943,930	7.95%	13.65%	53.18%
4	13,579,713	16,710,230	35,943,930	7.95%	13.69%	37.68%
5	14,659,300	19,019,330	35,943,930	7.95%	13.75%	29.15%
10	21,489,508	36,525,140	48,943,680	7.95%	13.84%	17.24%
15	31,502,114	70,617,360	86,153,180	7.95%	13.91%	15.44%
20	46,179,894	136,575,200	158,427,200	7.95%	13.95%	14.82%
30	99,238,319	525,828,200	552,119,600	7.95%	14.13%	14.32%
40	213,258,263	2,004,725,000	2,104,961,000	7.95%	14.17%	14.31%

At the death of the insured, the insurer will pay out the policy death benefit income tax free (which includes the value of the insurance dedicated fund account) to the beneficiary designated by the owner of the policy. During the life of the insured, the policy can be cashed in for an amount equal to the value of the insurance dedicated fund (IDF) without the imposition of surrender charges (that would normally apply in a traditional life insurance policy), or the owner of the policy may access cash value via the use of loans taken against the policy.

The cash value of the PPLI policy is increased by the investment performance and yields on the IDF managed account assets, without any erosion for income taxes. The cost of setting up this type of policy (including issuance costs, servicing fees, etc.) will generally be significantly less than the first year's income tax savings on the IDF returns.

Annual charges, excluding the cost of the insurance protection, will be between 85 and 125 basis points. In return for the willingness to assume these costs, the policy owner and the beneficiaries will not be subject to current taxation of the inside build-up of the policy cash value (the separately managed investment fund value and accumulated earnings). Moreover, if the policy is maintained until the death of the insured, the entire death benefit will be received by the beneficiary free of all U.S. income taxes, including all of the earnings from the IDF from inception of the policy.

Estate Planning with PPLI

If the ownership of the policy is properly

structured and the insured has no control over the policy or incidents of ownership, the policy death benefit will be exempt from the federal estate tax. The net benefit of sheltering the investment income and accumulations from income and estate tax is the equivalent of a 400% + incremental rate of return (in any given year) on investment vis-à-vis the ownership of income and estate taxable investments.[1] The compounding effect of this incremental advantage produces much larger advantages over time.

As a part of the estate planning process, PPLI offering policy investment options may prove to be the appropriate solution to help meet a variety of objectives. PPLI is effectively an institutionally priced or "no- load" life insurance policy with very sophisticated investment options.

---

[1]The benefit of the policy insulated growth of the account, based upon a 47% average combined income tax rate levied on traditional taxable investment compounded over the life of the investor plus the estate tax rate of 40% which would be levied on the fund balance at the death of the account holder, provides a combined net after - tax value of the policy which is approximately four times the value of the

non-insurance investment account.

Clearly, for these individuals, the issue of funding the payment of the estate tax is extremely important. Wealthy individuals are faced with the imposition of a 40% tax (in 2015) on the assets that they wish to leave to children, grandchildren and other loved ones. An investment vehicle, with a substantial income and estate tax free death benefit (PPLI), can provide the necessary liquidity for the payment of estate taxes.

PPLI vs. Traditional Cash Value Life Insurance

For those wealthy individual investors who currently have traditional cash value life insurance policies (whole life or universal life), the possibility of securing a more aggressive investment alternative and a lower cost structure for their life insurance may be available. These existing policies may be exchanged for new policies without the imposition of income tax on the accumulated earnings within the policy.

The Internal Revenue Code enables owners of such policies the opportunity to exchange them for new policies on an income tax-free basis provided that the rules of Section 1035 and the individual State regulations are complied with. Section 1035 provides that an existing insurance policy may be exchanged for a new insurance policy on the same insured providing all of the Federal and State formalities attendant to the exchange are completed between the insurance companies involved with the exchange.

These rules enable the exchange to occur with no cash coming into the hands of the policy owner at any time during the process. For example, it may, therefore, be possible for the wealthy investor with significant existing cash value life insurance that is owned in an irrevocable life insurance trust to seek the cooperation of the trustees of that trust in converting the existing policies into insurance policies that will provide enhanced benefits to family members. It is very important to note that these trusts may be useful in providing the beneficiaries with income and support benefits during the life of the insured patriarch or matriarch. However, the insured is subject to medical underwriting requirements. The existing policy should not be exchanged until the new insurance offer is in place.

One of the failures of traditional life insurance trust planning is that there is generally limited availability of funds to provide lifetime benefits because of the cost structure, and investment performance. It is not uncommon for the grantor/insured under such a trust to complain that there are no benefits available for their children "until I die".

PPLI with its potentially superior investment performance and lower cost structure is uniquely suited to meet the income needs of this grantor by enabling more aggressive investments that may increase cash accumulations which can be accessed as policy loans during their lifetime without compromising the integrity of the death benefits which the policy is designed to produce.
These same policy loans combined with loans from the trust to the grantor (or in the case of integrated estate planning asset protection trusts, a discretionary power in the trustee to pay trust accounting income (not necessarily subject to tax) or principal to the grantor) can provide the means to secure lifetime access to the IDF investment accumulation account for the grantor.

IRC Section 7702A provides that a modified endowment contract ("MEC") is a life insurance policy which is over-funded in the initial years of its existence based upon the timing and amount of premiums paid in relation to its death benefit. The MEC rules are essentially designed to discourage policy premium front- loading in the manner in which Congress believes too closely resembles the way an investor would make his or her investment in an annuity product.

The following unfortunate repercussions arise following characterization of a life insurance policy as a MEC:

- Loans taken from or secured by the policy are generally deemed to be distributions of earnings from the policy.
- All distributions, including payments upon the lapse or surrender of a MEC policy, are generally taxable as ordinary income up to the amount by which the cash surrender value of the policy exceeds the cumulative amount of premiums paid into the policy.
- A 10 percent additional income tax is imposed on all distributions made prior to the insured attaining age 59½; provided, however, that this penalty shall not apply

where the insured is disabled, or where such distributions are part of a series of substantially equal periodic payments extending over the life of the taxpayer.

Where an insurance policy is not characterized as a MEC, loans can generally be made from the policy on a "tax-free" basis. This result will ordinarily still be achieved in cases where the cumulative loans are in excess of the cumulative premiums paid into the policy. However, in the event of a lapse of the policy, the loan amounts will become taxable to the extent that they are in excess of the policy cost basis.

The policy's cost basis is its cumulative premiums. Loans and partial surrender of the cash value are the primary mechanism, whereby the policy owner is permitted to have access to a portion of the investment account during the insured's lifetime. As such, non-MEC status is of critical importance in order to obtain the full benefits of this planning.

The determination of whether a life insurance policy is a MEC is based on complex actuarial calculations and what is known as the "seven-pay" test. Generally, a policy is a MEC where, for example, the cumulative premiums paid at any time during the first seven years of the contract exceed the sum of the maximum net level premiums that could have been paid on or before such time, if the contract provided for paid-up future benefits after the payment of seven level annual premiums.

Effectively, this test requires that the premiums paid into the policy be made over several years, as opposed to a single up-front payment. The seven-pay test, through complex actuarial assumptions and calculations, can be passed for a premium payment period of only five years (sometimes, even less).

Frozen Cash Value Life Insurance

Frozen cash value life insurance ("FCV") is best known as a flexible premium variable adjustable (universal) life insurance policy that is issued by offshore life insurance companies domiciled in tax-haven jurisdictions such as Bermuda or the Cayman Islands. Recently, a two-specialty life insurer has emerged in Puerto Rico that offers both traditional PPLI as well as FCV policies.

The policy is intentionally designed to violate IRC Sec 7702, the Internal Revenue Code tax law definition of life insurance. The other legal considerations are imposed under the insurance laws of the jurisdiction where the coverage is issued. Generally speaking, all of the carriers issue the coverage as variable life insurance.

In the beginning, FCV policies were only issued by life insurers that had not made the election under IRC Sec 953(d) to be treated as a U.S. taxpayer. This election is important since the life insurer's separate account is treated as a non-resident alien for income tax purposes. Without the election, certain categories of investment income would be subject to withholding taxation under IRC Sec 871(a) at a 30.0% rate. Recently, several life insurers have started issuing FCV policies in their IRC Sec 953(d) electing companies.

Under most FCV contracts, the death benefit is equal to the sum of guaranteed specified amount of death benefit plus the cash value on the claim date plus the policy's mortality reserve value on the claim date. This amount is essentially the cumulative premiums plus or minus investment experience along with a death benefit corridor which most carriers express as a fixed percentage between 102.5% to 110.0%. A Puerto Rican life insurer referenced above, issues policies with a fixed amount of coverage ($1 million) above the initial premium and mortality reserve.

The cash value under most FCV policies is defined as the fair market value of all assets constituting the policy fund, less any policy loans and less any accrued unpaid fees or expenses due under the terms of the policy. The "Cash Surrender Value" of the of the Policy is the lesser of (a) the cash value or (b) the sum of all premiums paid under the Policy, computed without regard to, any surrender charges, and policy loans, under the terms of the Policy.

The cash value increases or decreases depending upon the investment experience of the policy fund. FCV policies do not provide for or guarantee any minimum cash value. The insurer holds the appreciation of the assets (in excess of the amount of cumulative premiums) held in the separate account as a mortality reserve within the insurer's separate account solely for the purposes of funding the payment of the death benefit payable under the FCV policy.

Under most FCV contracts, the policyholder may

take a tax-free partial surrender of the policy cash value up to the amount of cumulative premiums within the policy. The policyholder may also take a policy loan up to 90.0% of the policy's cumulative premiums. The policy loan terms will vary from company to company. The significance of a partial surrender versus a policy loan is that the partial surrender will not leave the policy with a liability. The surrender and loan proceeds are tax-free under any circumstance and provide the policyholder with access to policy assets on a tax-free basis.

The tax authority for FCV policies is very straightforward. Several large national law firms have opined favorably on this type of policy. The legal analysis is straightforward in IRC Sec 7702(g). The policyholder is taxed on any inside buildup of the cash value and mortality charges except that the policy definition does not provide for any inside buildup. The mortality corridor is also very small. IRC Sec 7702(g) states that a tax-defective policy still receives income tax-free treatment for the death benefit under IRC Sec 101(a).

One way to look at the FCV policy is that it is effectively like a variable deferred annuity only with better taxation for the taxpayer. Similarly, it is like a Modified Endowment Contract (MEC) without being subject to the MEC rules.

FCV policies are extremely efficient for accumulating wealth with a minimal cost "drag" due to the policy's mortality cost for the net amount at risk in the policy. Whether a carrier has a fixed percentage corridor of 105-110 percent or a fixed amount corridor of $1 million, the FCV policy is very efficient for wealth accumulation purposes. The death benefit ultimately delivers the investment accumulation in excess of the initial premium on a tax-free basis. The policyholder is able to take loans from the FCV policy on a tax-free basis in an amount equal to 90% of his cumulative premiums in case the taxpayer needs to access his investment.

The policy is well suited for taxpayers whose single premium would exceed the available reinsurance capacity for an insured. This amount is believed to be approximately $65 million on a worldwide basis. The tax-free death benefit is a much stronger result that the taxation of a deferred annuity at death.

Conclusion

PPLI is an exciting solution to many of the concerns of the wealthy. It provides a low cost flexible platform for individuals who are looking for a tax advantaged solution for tax inefficient investments. It provides a life insurance benefit to heirs on an income tax free basis and if the contract is set up properly, it can provide a tax advantaged income stream.

PPLI can be a valuable addition to your overall investment and insurance portfolio provided proper structures are established and proper procedures are followed. PPLI is still largely under-utilized by high net worth investment investors and provides an excellent opportunity to enhance the after-tax return of one's investments while addressing a number of other tax and estate planning issues at the same time.

Biographies

Gerry Nowotny is a tax and estate planning attorney in Avon, CT.
Gerry has a JD and LL.M in estate planning from the University of Miami School of Law. He has his undergraduate degree from the United States Military Academy. He served on  active duty for five years and left the service as a Captain. He has completed the CLU, ChFC and CFP designations.

Gerry has developed a national reputation in certain niche tax planning strategies such as private placement insurance products. He is well published in tax and estate planning periodicals.

Roey Diefendorf is a 45 year veteran wealth manager in Locust Valley, NY.
Roey has a Masters in Insurance from Georgia State University. He has his undergraduate degree from Bucknell University in

Psychology and has completed the CLU, ChFC, RFC, CFP, CIMA and CAP designations.

Roey has developed his national reputation in the "total" wealth management arena with the introduction of two books *"3 Dimensional Wealth: A Radically Sane Perspective On Wealth Management"* and *"A Better Way: Using Purposeful Trusts To Preserve Values & Valuables In Perpetuity"*.

Roey founded both Argonne Trust Company, Inc. (SD) and the Monroe Insurance Dedicated Funds (DE) bringing values based solutions to the domestic PPLI marketplace.

For More Information:
>**3 Dimensional Wealth Advisory, LLC**
>152 Forest Avenue, Locust Valley, NY 11560
>1-877-3D-Wealth

3 DIMENSIONAL
WEALTH ADVISORY

Made in the USA
Middletown, DE
29 July 2017